ECHOES OF OUR FATHERS

Humble Beginnings

written by **OTHIR BRISTER**

ISBN # 979-8-9882754-2-8
PUBLISHED BY BLACKCURRANT PRESS COMPANY. ALL RIGHTS RESERVED.
COPYRIGHT (C) BY Othir Brister.
ALL RIGHTS RESERVED.

Graphic Cover Design: Neville McDowell
Editor: C. Lewis

www.blackcurrantpress.com

ECHOES OF OUR FATHERS

Humble Beginnings

Written By
OTHIR BRISTER

SPECIAL DEDICATION

A soul of a person can harvest many, thoughts, emotions, feeling, ideas, regrets, and sorrows,so the idea of folding your hand will always sit at the back of your mind. To achieve what's achievable one must sometimes bend, but never break.

When times get ruff we'll look to the skies, then fall to our knees in prayer. When hope seems lost we'll return to our prayer rooms and knees once again to the foot of the cross.

On a man's knees he preys "God grant me the serenity to accept the things I cannot change, courage to change things I can, and wisdom to know the difference."

So I dedicate this book to the person who is the hammer to my nail in making me kneel to these facts:

Therefore I say unto you, what things soever ye desire, when ye pray, believe that ye receive them, and ye shall receive them.
                              - NEW TESTAMENT: MARK, XI, 23, 24

LOVE YOU, MOM aka JOANN BRISTER

ACKNOWLEDGEMENT
We all hear voices that echo from the mind, a sense of should I or shouldn't I. The rationalization of right or wrong, but when one though is concorded over the other that's what will make your character. But, also that parent that left that everlasting echo, that word that stood out to you will forever ring in your mind. An echo!

FOREWARD

Learn what an echo is all our life's, and from birth we've listened to people, mom, dad, sister's, brother's, neighbors, class mate, unconsciously learning what people do. Words spoken that echoed around in your head until one day you had to use them. These words would stay in the back of your mind until you brought them forth. No matter what type of school you attended it will teach you to echo words from the back of your mind. One of your first homework's as a child was to write some words multiple time so it would echo in the back of your mind. After storing this word to use at a later date you would move on to other words, than larger words, than you had to pull out the dictionary.

Echos are simple that storage place between the eyes and the brain.

Stage one of the echos began when mom said no. You tried her, you did it again. She planted that echo by saying "Do it again an I'm gonna pop you!" You did it again and got popped. Now, as you cried you associated that pain with the echo of "No!" So now when you reach for it again you know what will happen. To learn no as one of your first echo words set boundaries for a lifetime to come.

No means no, no matter where you are!

NOTE TO SELF

Many individuals interchange the words "hearing" and "listening" and mistake them for the same meaning. The definition of hearing revolves around the physiological act of hearing sounds.

The definition of listening revolves around actively paying attention to the words and sounds that you hear to absorb their meaning.

Francis Barraud's

PREFACE

As a father I learned from my father that I had only one job. To provide for my family and take care of my children by any means necessary. This was the echo that rang through my mind on a daily bases. When I woke in the mornings, during the day, and as I laid my head down at night. It said,"Take care of your family as I have taken care of you!"

Echo by definition:

A sound or series of sounds caused by a reflection of sound waves from a surface back to the listener.

TABLE OF CONTENTS

JOANN BRISTER

AFTERWORDS

Life itself is about learning lessons. From the womb to the tomb as I've heard it. But are we learning for the moment, or learning to utilize it at a later date?

As a son, be eager to learn everything!

If your pop fixes something around the house watch, learn how! If pop is confronted by anyone watch how he handles it. Watch how pop takes care of the family. You can learn how you want you family to be taken care of. Learn that you have to forgive him for short coming because sometimes the burdens of his environment might have brought about problems for him. But watch him, there will always be a lesson.

Remember, be a solution to the problem, not the problem.

CHAPTER 1
Who are you?

Do you know or will you ever know who you are?

You wake up one morning and you say to yourself. I need more! More money, more excitement, I just need to make people understand "The me." Ok, the idea is there now how do you implement it. You need a spiritual moment with yourself. Go sit by some water, any place where it's quiet. Then listen. Take in all the universe has to offer.

Now step one is complete. That's all you ever needed. To learn that if your environment is moving to fast. Slow it down, take yourself out of the equation. Find your quiet place. Now your new being begins.

Most people never learn to slow themselves down. Always saying "I got too much going on"! But it's your life! If you don't control your life, your life will control you!

WHAT MAKES YOU YOU?

A person could be anything they want. If you sing in the shower, your a singer. Not a professional singer, but a singer. If you work on your own car, your a mechanic not a professional mechanic. This entire philosophy brings about the notion of you are what people see you doing or who you train yourself to be.

Inside of you there are many different emotions, abilities, behaviors, attitudes, the control of these come from you and only you. Figure out how much power you want to exert in each area. This will build your to who your going to be.

KNOW YOUR STRENGTHS

In knowing your strengths you can surpass most obstacles. You alone will know your limits.

KNOW YOUR WEAKNESSES

In knowing your weaknesses you will know the areas where you may fall short so the extra is required. Example: Twice the training and some.

In doing these things you will find out that there's the you, then there's "The you!"

WHO DO YOU THINK YOU ARE?

By now you've done done some research of your history I hope? Asking question about your grand parents, your mom and pops earlier years, and your ancestors to get and idea of the cloths you were made from. Now you should have a faint picture of who you really are.

EMBRACE YOU

Add on what is needed to make you whole, the exercise for a fit body, the reading for knowledge, the spiritual guidance from above and carry it with you always.

Nobody tells us how to be men. We just are.
- Robert Jordan

The "I am!"
I am, in deed, a king
Because I know how to rule myself.
- Pietro Aretino

Be who you are and say what you feel, because those who mind don't matter, and those who matter don't mind.
~ Bernard M. Baruch

CHAPTER 2
High level of consciousness

If a young man starts to watch the world for answers they will come to him. They are out there waiting for him.

DREAM TO LEARN AND UNDERSTAND EVERYTHING. Every person, and why that person acts the way they do. We as people tend to jump to conclusions on why others react in a certain manor instead of examining the ourselves, and who we are first.

Only a few people look behind the eyes of others to see what they see. There are places where people are given medication for their action to keep them performing in a so called normal way. But, what is normal?

If and elevator is full of passengers facing the door and you get on facing the rear and stay that way society says your not normal.

Mainly because your going against the norms, or what society has deemed normal behavior.

Is Stephen Curry, Michael Jordan, or Hussein Bolt abnormal because their talents are exceptional. Food for thought. Could it be their bodies were developed in certain ways that all they had to do was zoom in and train themselves then their extreme talents would kick in.

I can't say that everyone has a talent. But, I can say that if you are a conscious person to what you do in this world it will open you up to a deeper understanding of who you are. Your like, dislikes, your self awareness of people, things around you, and what or how to stay away from.

It's like playing a game of pool. You get beat so many times that you learn the angles, the diamonds. The diamonds are placed on the table so that you can angle your balls in certain pockets. Seeing the world is the same. But nothing is always the same. Your approach to figuring things out will allow you to place angles on your situations in life. How you structure yourself to handle it is totally your plan. People with your best interest in hand will offer suggestions, but only you know you!

You are the light of the world, when your compassion radiates and pervades the world. When your mind is in higher consciousness and heart is full with compassion, your deeds will glorify the humanity and the Father in the heavens.
~ Amit Ray

CHAPTER 3
Conscious Decisions

YOU EITHER CONTROL YOUR LIFE, OR YOUR LIFE CONTROLS YOU.

CHOOSE THOUGHTS YOU COULD LIVE WITH
A sound mind is aways the way to go. If you have to look over your back because of something you did and couldn't correct or something your thinking about doing and it's not correct.

1. Correct what problems you may have.
2. Forget about doing something's that will interfere with your sleep at night.

AVOID THOUGHTS THAT CRIPPLE YOU
If someone's saying to you don't do it, think about it. If this will cause you any find of set back, then don't do it. The problem with most people is not listening until it's too late.

SAY NO WHEN IT DOESN'T FEEL RIGHT

Your environment plays a role in the opportunities you are faced with to do wrong. Most inner city kids see more opportunities to do wrong than kids from the suburbs. They see more going on in the streets. Their friends introduce them to many things. This is where your will as to who you are is challenged. Saying no to what you feel is wrong is the right thing to do.

RATIONALIZE YOUR THOUGHTS

Think! If I do this, that will happen! If I do that, this will happen!

DON'T BE COACHED INTO NOTHING

Friends persuasions. Some friends are true to the word friend. But others, might as well be enemies. They try and coach you into doing things with them and when you fall short they laugh. Watch those friend who laugh in your time of discomfort.

Stop saying what you want in life and go get it. JUST DO IT was the phrase. Where did that come from? A person just like you woke up one morning, looked in the mirror and and said "Enough!"

> Enough of being broke.
> Enough of living from check to check.
> Enough of struggling.
> If your "Enough" supersedes your "Just making it" then do something about it!

That pretty girl you sat next to in High School that all the guys were attached to, but she wouldn't give them the time of day. But she made it her business to always talk to you. You would always talk about her but never pursue her. Now you've graduated.

A thought without action is just a thought.

Nobody's life is ever all balanced.
It's a conscious decision to choose your priorities every day.
~ Elisabeth Hasselbeck

In any moment of decision, the best thing you can do is the right thing, the next best thing is the wrong thing, and the worst thing you can do is nothing.
~ Theodore Roosevelt

CHAPTER 4
The Dreamer

DARE TO DREAM

A dreamer sees things differently. His angles are different. His approach to conquering his dream is also different.

Many care to dream but dreams with no action are only dreams. A man once said that in his dreams he seen things that he desired. So when he woke up he wrote it on paper. As he wrote it on paper he began to think of it on a daily basis until it became an obsession. His obsession ate on him daily so it had to be satisfied. And so he satisfied his obsession.

If you can eat, sleep and dream anything not only will you want it badly, but you will guarantee yourself it.

DESERVE THE DREAM

If anyone deserves to have it you do. Don't sell yourself short. Stop saying how can I get that, or can I afford that. That's to much for me.

If this world is the world that we all hope it is, and we place the energy in the air that we desire something, and when it comes you don't claim it. Shame on you. Energy wasted. That blessing could have gone to someone else. Someone who needed more.

BLOCKING BLESSINGS

Getting in your own way. Telling others of your dream before the dream is complete. Talking to much. Hate in your heart and won't let it go. Reasoning with hatred. It take so much energy to hate. Why do it at all! These are some reasons your dreams get block.

STAYING LOCKED IN

The Rapper Meek Mill stated "There are three types of people in this world!"

1. Those who make it happen.
2. Those who watch it happen.
3. And those who don't know what's happening.

If your going to dream, dream big!

If your desires , wants, needs are determined by your 24 hours in a day, then use your 24 hours wisely.

A person will say dare to dream about something, but places no effort behind it.

The statement stands, but the effort is lacked.

Grave yards are full of dreamers. Don't be another forgotten tombstone.

All men dream, but not equally. Those who dream by night in the dusty recesses of their minds, wake in the day to find that it was vanity: but the dreamers of the day are dangerous men, for they may act on their dreams with open eyes, to make them possible.
-T. E. Lawrence

CHAPTER 5
Temptations

We've all been tempted at one point or another. It's one of the very special choices in a humans DNA. It makes you who you are. It actual makes you draw a line between what you will and will not do.

Temptation's are best known for their attacks on people of these qualities: trustworthy, loyal, and obedient individuals.

RELIGION TEMPTATION

No matter what the religion temptation stands by and try to provoke you into doing something against what is being taught. The reason for studying your scriptures.

STREET TEMPTATION

The many temptations of the streets: Foods you shouldn't be eating. You know it's poisonous to your system, so you say I'll just have a little and, a little bit won't heart!

Alcohol or drugs that take over your system. You'll never know what their capable of until your addicted and need more.

Women, until you've caught some that either you have to live with or it kills you then you'll know you should have resisted.

Sweets, going to the dentist wasn't enough.

He told you to lay off the sweets, and now those Implants are costing you a future.

Gambling, you couldn't resist now your home is being repossessed. Leaving you saying if only I listened to my X-Wife.

That fast car, the ride of all rides. It was fast I couldn't resist racing until the day I swerved an hit that tree. Now I'm being fed through a straw.

That pretty girl, down the block who never told you she was married. Her husband came home and almost caught you before you jump out the third floor window. Now you walk with a lip the rest of your life.

Mans greatest temptations:
1. Women
2. Money
3. Substance (Alcohol included)

Watch and pray so that you will not fall into temptation. The spirit is willing, but the body is weak.

MATTHEW 26:41

Nothing can save you from that which you are not willing to give up.
- C. Fantelli

CHAPTER 6
Revenge

The best revenge is massive success.
- Frank Sinata

Stop thinking thoughts that take you back. Move forward. Each time you choose to think about anything in a negative way your blessing are held back.

THINK ABOUT THIS!
People who choose to live in the negative who just want negativity in their lives sometimes develop a certain type of mental cancer. And I do believe it could be contagious. You will know if you catch it because you will start being negative yourself.

CLOSE THE DOOR ON SOME PEOPLE.
There are people that no matter what you do for them they will never act in accordance with the way you want them to. Learn and if their aren't for you then they are against you. At least keep

that in mind. Sometimes you have to clean house with people with certain attitudes, behaviors, problems, habits, jealousies. These things are brought to you and they become your issues also.

WATCH THE COMPANY YOU KEEP

If he tells a person something and he tells you something else watch him. He's a deceiver. A deceiver normally gets someone hurt or killed. This is his mission to put you in the line of fire. He doesn't care about you, your family, or anyone as long as he get personal gain.

ALWAYS FEEL WATCHED

Being paranoid is a wonderful thing. It keeps you on your toes, keep other's at bay, and keeps your development as a person sharp.

People can't double talk to you. Your able to get out the way when need be, and most of the time you'll see what ever is coming.

THE PLOT FOR REVENGE

So your plotting revenge on this person who wronged you. Now you can't sleep because it's happening. Their about to get what's coming to them. It happening. You rejoice bathing in glory. The person gets seriously hurt. Can't work anymore. You find out their have a child and are about to get thrown on the street. Was it worth it? How you feel? Did you accomplish what you wanted. Would it have been better to just avoid this person!

STREET JUSTICE

If you take to the street remember this, the street holds no loyalty to no one. You do what you do, and hold it to the back of your mind until that day it catches up to you. Then its time to pay the street back!

PRAYER JUSTICE

You will pray for your enemy, and wish him well in life. And hope that you never cross paths again, until that one day he'll see you in the street while with his friends, and you'll wish you've beat him down when he was alone!

Douglas Horton wrote, *"While seeking revenge, dig two graves - one for yourself."*

CHAPTER 7
Respect & represent the men before you

Our father's wishes were to have children that not only obeyed the laws of man, but the laws of the father. They knew that some day you could give it your all, and others days you would fall short ending up on your knees. But they also knew that by letting you show them what you were capable of, an in return they would pick up the slack.

Those wishes also included you respecting yourself as well as others.

How does a man who don't respect himself respect others? Not possible!

If you have no respect for yourself. Stay inside. Stay away from people. Your not only unpredictable, your dangerous.

We as father's didn't pull what we know out of the air, we learned from our father and try to create a better way of doing things so that you could have easier, and make it easier for your son, as well as his son.

Today our culture has grown so far away from "It takes a village to raise a child."

Or maybe the children of today done fell back on learning their history. Your history is your history for a reason. If anything it tells you who your people are. With that comes a broad number of strengths. You can get lost or confused in the everyday hustle of city life, but when your taught your history you learn to reach back and pull your strengths forward.

Our fathers only ask that you walking in a mans way, keep good hygiene, respect yourself as well as others. Honor you mother and father as they did. Protect your family and prosper. The basics!

Difference is the instinctive respect which we pay to the great and good; the unconscious acknowledgement of the superiority or excellence of others.
~ Tryon Edwards

CHAPTER 8
Reasoning

There is impulse, and reaction, before reasoning in most cases. People will react on impulse if there is emotion involved. Reasoning is a highly subjective thing. In order to reason you need time to think. In split second situations reasoning is thought of last. We all wish that we could think every situation through but given the time it's not possible.

Within reason is also a phrase used to limit a person reason or give the an excuse for not using the full reasoning tools.

REASONING AS A STATE OF MIND
You have to figure most people learn to reason when they get a certain age, because if not the prisons would be running over. Not saying that some of the people didn't use reasoning before they committed the crime just saying that there are more criminals who used less reasoning to commit their crimes.

Reasoning is more on the scale of rational thoughts. If you

reason for a point of time and have a fairly good up bring then you become a rational thinker. But if you reason with an less fortunate up bringing then your irrational thinking take point.

THERE'S NO REASONING WITH YOU

A person that can't be reasoned with is a selfish person and can't be trusted. Their way is always the right way! It's their way or the highway.

The person chooses to do things their way no matter what. They will tell you that we have done this this way for years and they still do it their way.

There is another type of person one who listens, who's reasoning allows him to acknowledge what is going on, collects what being said to propose a solution at a later day. The mind of a positive reasoning person collect reasonable ideas from everyone, look over them, propose the best idea.

CHOOSE REASONING OVER CONFLICT

Most problems can be resolved by conversation. Most conflicts escalate because reasoning is lost. If we reasoned to the point where we agree to except 50 percent of the blame, then there is no conflict.

HOW WE MOVE

For some reason people believe that when something is said to them they must react in a certain way. What dictates this would be the environment. If your in a hostile environment, or less fortunate environment you tend to react aggressively. The environment teaches you to adapt to the people surrounding you. This changes the actual you. If there are friends who want to game and smoke to wee hours of the morning and get up late for work. Know that that's not you unless you want it to be you. He probably has a plan, and you following his plan will lead you straight down that dark whole. So I'll tell you this, second place is always reserved for someone.

True courage is a result of reasoning.
A brave mind is always impregnable.
Jeremy Collier

CHAPTER 9
Selfishness

Know this. It's not easy being a mom or a dad. Children look at it as if you brought me into the world you take care of me. Yes, that's partially correct. Until you can fin for yourself most parents will do that. The problem is! At what age is that?

As parents we understand that your going to try certain things, we understand that we must let you fall sometimes in order that you should know what the pavement feels like. But, we also know that we have to pick you up sometimes and dust you off and say try it again.

It seems to us parents that there are children who go get what they want and others who sit back and let things come to them. If you wish to have anything you desire in life go get it. The same rules apply. If you fall, pick yourself up, dust yourself off, and try again.

Try and put yourself in position to be able to help someone else.

Especially mom and pop. Remember those late nights spent on the games, remember those half hour showers, that warm dry room, those holy sneakers and that hungry stomach. It wasn't easy for them but they made away because they were taught the same things your being taught.

It's important that the revolving door keeps revolving. You must teach the next generation what you've been taught. Of course it won't be easy because as time progresses the robotic world will eliminate many things. This will cause people to become lazy, obesity, and more prone to sickness.

It's always a good practice to help those who groomed you into the person you have become. They have paved the way with words of encouragement, acts of kindness, even comforting you when you were ill. If nothin else they deserve to see that you understood what they were doing.

Self-centered people have only one thing to talk about-
themselves.
- Stef Harder

CHAPTER 10
Tough Love

A part of what makes us is the restrictions we get from mom and pop as a child. There were times when you didn't know better, and there were times you tried them. You really didn't know at an early age that if you threw your bottle on the ground you had to pick it up. You did it for a while, you thought it was fun, they thought it was cute. But after they got tired of laughing, having fun, it wasn't funny anymore grown ups get tired of kneeling down. So the training started. Pick it up they said. Pick it up or get popped. You tried them at first, but seeing their hand go up you knew it could only be bad for you. You didn't want the pop so you picked it up.

So your in your teens now, and they tell you don't hang out pass 11:00pm. You figure what can they do if I come in at 1:00am. You get home and the doors are locked. You knock, there's no answer. You call, no answer. You call a friend and shack up for the night.

You borrow the family car on occasions to hang out. Your parents realize that each time you bring the car back the gas hands on empty. Saturday's the big date. You ask for the car and the answer is no.

Tough love is brutally honest and hurts you to help you. Tough love cuts you when you're already bruised and berates you when you don't heal faster.
- Helen Hoang

REMEMBER IT'S NOT ALWAYS ABOUT YOU!

CHAPTER 11
Discipline & Constraint

*Success is the result of nothing more than a few simple
disciplines, practiced everyday.*
- Jim Rohn

If my desire is to stop drinking I would discipline myself to take
a scenic route away from the liquor store, and constrain myself
from going to bars. In doing so I learn to resist the urge of
alcohol.

CHAPTER 12
Last minute

LATENESS IS NEVER ACCEPTED

No matter where you go in life being late will never be accepted. You training to not be late starts at an earlier age in school. Most schools would have you go to the Dean's Office an sit an wait until the next point or would make you wait outside the classroom for that teacher talk. Teachers talks were like threats, no one liked teachers talks because they would always bring your parents into it. And you never wanted your parents involved. This was the early teaching of don't be late. Little did we know there was a larger picture.

When your late for anything some else's time is thrown off cause a domino affect. Example: Mom is taking me to school tomorrow so I have to get up early. I was gaming last night and forgot to set my alarm clock so I'm late she's yelling. She's now driving recklessly to get me to school so she don't be late for work. She gets to work late and her co-worker has a few choices words for her because she had to be at her other job at a certain time. You see how this affect multiple people. All because you weren't responsible enough to put school before the gaming.

BETTER AN HOUR EARLY THEN TWO MINUTES LATE
People wanna know how responsible you are when it comes to their time. If you say your gonna be there at a certain time, be there! Just as sure as your time is valuable to you their time is valuable to them. How would you like waiting an hour over the time someone gives you. Most of the time it's not an hour you wait but it might as well be. Twenty minutes will feel like an hour sometimes.

The best practice for this is to be and hour early rather then two minutes late. Why?

The person who is always cutting it close has to rush daily, time is no real factor in their lives. Their figure they can talk their way out of a pink slip or maybe they feel someones looking out for them. This will one day come to an end. Either they will get fired for tardiness or the person who they thought had their back no longer could cover for them.

The person who chooses to be an hour early will alway be relaxed, having breakfast, organizing, no choice words coming from their co-worker, the start of their day is always pleasant because there's no strain on time. No boss calling them into the office to reprimand them. Not having to leave work with a headache. Choose which character you want to be.

RUSHING TO CATCH UP

No one likes a person who's always rushing. First of all it's danger to the person as well as to others. Rushing doesn't allow a person to think clearly. It adds pressure to what's being done. You already knew what you had to do, so why didn't you give yourself the proper time. No it's time to play catch up and it's the Holidays were you get twice the work load.

TIME IS EVERYTHING

You loose every time not putting time first. Your event for the next day should be time set the night before. Your work schedule set the night before. Everything, is aways the night before. If you chose to go on a cruise with friends it would probably be plan weeks before and you can structure your life the night before.

Being young you should have that wake up energy. Wake up and flip out of bed ready for the day.

Stop being in the nick of time and be on time.

Time waits for no man!

> *If it weren't for the last minute,*
> *Nothing would get done.*
> *- Rita Mae Brown*

> *You may delay, but time will not.*
> *~ Benjamin Franklin*

CHAPTER 13
Walk in the shadow of men

Men who have paved the way who gave there lives for you to walk free today should always be honored. From chains to a free world we came. Women who took chance of utility being assaulted, abused, or killed. Men who stared in the face of guns, risked being dragged by a horse, escaped being hung by ropes put their lives on the line so that you would have a better future.

Some went to their death just to prove a point, others refusing to be treated a certain way. It's for children of today to understand back then because there are no teaching of this anymore. And when you do here it, it comes out of a Rapper's mouth the wrong way "Slavery was a choice"! This statement along took us back one hundred years. If you don't know what your talking about don't say nothing. Because, the younger generations who hears this may grasp on to it and start believing the non truth.

For a man to go back in his history restore power to himself and his existing family, an extended families to come. The words spoken by the father of the father's before him gives strength to the sons who in return strengthen their families and sons.

Your history is very important this is why a people would try and eliminate it from the school.
Don't just take this information from me,
LOOK IT UP!

> *Waste no time arguing about what a*
> *good man should be. Be one.*
> *- Marcus Aurelius*

CHAPTER 14
Move different

For some reason some people believe that when something is said to them they must react in a certain way id dictated to them by there environment. If your in a hostile environment, or less fortunate environment you tend to get angered quick.

The environment teaches you to adapt to those around you. Which changes or dictate to you how you should be. Example: If my friend smokes substance and is lazy to get up the next morning due to gaming all night and I might not smoke but I gamed with him all night his influence buried who I am.

Your own thoughts. Your own state of mind should always be your goal. A limit on the funs of life to enhance great decisions for on coming years.

My friend calls me to game at 9:00pm, I tell him I only have a few hours. I can no longer spend 6 hours playing I have other responsibilities. A real friend understands. A fake friend will probably look to someone else to keep up at night.

Think about it! What more important having this person as a friend, or being able to get what ever you want in life.

The thing is, you don't know your friend's plans. Maybe their have time like that.
YOU DO!!!

When I let go of what I am, I become what I might be. When I let go of what I have, I receive what I need.

- Lao Tzu

CHAPTER 15
Find better ways

Always reach for more pay in a good job or your own business. Don't just get a job your not satisfied with and stay there for years. It makes you miserable. Most times people get jobs and then fall into enjoying their coworkers so much that years pass and before they know it their 65. Start your plan early try and think about you first. The money is out there you just have to go get it.

PROBLEM INCREASE AS YOU AGE
Becoming responsible has his fees also! As you age the small responsibilities become larger responsibilities. Mean, when you were small you got feed, as you get older it's time to feed yourself, and maybe a family. You'll appreciate having more. And that's what growing up is all about.

CASH GOES UP AND DOWN
Learn that you don't need to keep up with the Joanses. You can get anything you want in due time. If you put money away for a

rainy day, which is sure to come you will be ahead of the game. The problems in some of our communities is something comes out and everyone wants it. They will spend their last to get it and then their saving is gone. Then something else comes out and the cycle continues. You had it, but you chose to be down instead.

EMERGENCY FUNDS

If you plan correctly there will always be emergency funds. Funds that were set aside for that rainy day. Like I said that rainy day will definitely come.

These funds are not just for emergencies but for days your car break down, your children may need school items, your wife my need extra money for a bill. Better to have it, then not.

BILLS DON'T STOP

Alway remember if you get in a bind with bills and haven't saved for that rainy day, bills don't care, they won't stop. But that rainy day money may hold you down until your luck increases. In the back of your mined there should always be a foot note saying what happens if My job lays me off or I am faced with an injury or sick how do I or my family survive the storm.

TWO HEADS TOGETHER

The cost of everything in certain cities continues to increase. How do you keep up?

Stop thinking you always have to do things alone. If you have a companion sit with this companion and discuss ways of increasing your financial opportunities. You both may benefit. Two heads are always better then one. Better yet two incomes are better then one.

.

CHAPTER 16
Get tired of being sick and tired

HAVE YOU HAD ENOUGH

Tired of not having enough money, tired of buses, trains, subway. Tired of rushing because someone else has to get you there. Then do something about it. Get up off that couch, stop doing things that are secondary to your life, and make a stand.

CHANGE

There's only one person in this world who understands you like you do, and that's you!

To ask another person to take care of your problems would be ridiculous. Change comes when except your problems and are will to take responsibility of them and handle them.

Stop beating a dead horse. People who say they're going to do something to better their lives should stick to the script.

Some will tell you to your face what they're gonna do to better their lives and every time you see them they say the same thing but never make a move. "You can lead a horse to water but you can't make him drink it I always said!"

STAND TEN TOES DOWN

Don't let people walk all over you. Let them know you have a switch. Let them know that how they treat you will be how you treat them. Nothing more nothing less.

ENOUGH IS ENOUGH

Only you know when enough is enough.
We will try an be civilized until you show me that your not.

START FROM TODAY

My goals are to acquire all my needs, my finance will accelerate.
I'd like to be mentally strong and morally correct.

Oprah Winfrey once said, *"You can have it all. You just can't have it all at once."*

CHAPTER 17
Money or power doesn't make the man

The corrupting influence of money and power over men. Man has started his individual walk against his brother. He desires more, and more now.

Back in the days we shared everything. But when he places himself in an environment where more is better, he changes. Money or power becomes his desires. He know that first he gets the money then he gets the power. It is said that money doesn't make the man and I believe it may try, but you will never know the man if he's in his position with that money.

It's important for a man to stay who he is after having nothing how many lower class people are at his feet. Not saying he will look down on them, just saying he won't see them the same way. On one hand he'd say "I made it" and the other hand saying "The creator did this!"

This is way we said be careful of the bridges you burn on the way up, it will be the same bridges on the way down.

FEELING POWERFUL

Feeling power is not the same as "That Powerful Feeling." A "Power" feeling could be an overwhelming urge, desire.

SELF-CONTROL

Nothing gives one person so much advantage over another as to remain always cool and unruffled under all circumstances.
- Thomas Jefferson

HERE THEY COME

Money or power both draws people to you, especially friends. When you had nothing you had limited friends. Now your somebody and everybody wants you. It's hard to learn to say no. But when you were down "No" was said to you frequently. So if you plan to keep what you have learn to say "No." Remember that once you had nothing, now you have something. I'm sure you like the something better.

HATERS

Frowned on by others is a way of life. Haters gonna hate. Being envied by some will also be a part of the hate but leave all of that on their shoulders. You can't change the faces of people who start to look at you differently.

Respect your efforts, respect yourself. Self-respect leads to self-discipline. When you have both firmly under your belt, that's
real power.
- Clint Eastwood

CHAPTER 18
Matter to mind

Learn to control yourself in all aspects of your body by utilizing your mind. You've heard mind, body, and spirit. These three together working as one. A force that takes you to another level.

Many will ask, "How do I do that?"

The example would be. The person that loved playing basketball. He got in a car accident and is now confined to a wheelchair.

His mind told him to give up. His spirit wouldn't allow him to, so he joyed a handicapped basketball team. Now, he's doing well. No sense of giving up, satisfying his urge to play basketball. His mind no longer attacks him due to his missing limbs. His body is exhausting that satisfying energy, and his spirit is running high on "If I'm doing this what else can I accomplish!"

Your body can stand anything, it's your mind you have to convince.
- Fredrich Nietzche

CHAPTER 19
Regrets

Regret is distress of the mind, sorrow for what has been done or failed to be done.

Regret by definition implies pain caused by deep disappointment, fruitless longing, or unavailing remorse.

There's not a person alive who doesn't have regrets. Regrets come with time lived. Looking back and saying either I could have done some different in my earlier time or saying this can be done another way but I did it this way.

It seems that if a person has no regrets they would be living a perfect life.

Of all sad words of tongue or pen, the saddest are these: "It might have been."
~ John Greenleaf Whittier

CHAPTER 20
Recognizing the most high

THE FATHER OF ALL FATHERS
The cultures, or language might differ but it's all in recognition of one.

Many people around the word stand at the foot of the cross. Welcoming his holy name.

Praying for strength to survive in this fierce world, strength for their families and their futures.

Some Preyer phrases used:
Oh god
God help us
Old great one
Son of the living god
Oh god help me
Jesus take the wheel
Jesus

Jesus Christ
Father help us
Father God
Bless it Jesus
All mighty
Praise his holy name

These are all phrases which recognize a high power. You must have used one of these in your life time, so you recognize someone greater than yourself.

When you realize Gods purpose for your life isn't just about you, he will use you in a mighty way.
- Dr. Tony Evans

CHAPTER 21
Good deeds are recognized.

A smile is probably the greatest gift a human being can give to another.

In an everyday life we're so busy trying to work and make money that we forget about the small things in life. A smile to a stranger could change their life and enhance your.

Think about it! It takes nothing to smile but yet in still people who lack smiling most of the time create a chemical change in their bodies that causes stress, and we know that stress leads to a variety of issues.

TO GIVE

At one time or another everyone has given something to a less fortunate person. Maybe the guy standing outside the store, maybe the woman who comes between the cars with her baby strapped to her back, or maybe the kid who sleeps on the sidewalk with his covers over his head. Although these are extreme cases, these are things we think of when we think of giving.

CHURCHES

The deeds of a church are of keeping mankind balanced. It welcomes all so that evil should never prevail. That being said, no one knows who's evil until something happens and the incident goes against mankind so it would be labeled evil.

The Churches role is to teach you to get in line with your spiritual self. If you can get in line with your spiritual self then you can connect spiritually with others. The reason to get together with multiple people of the same mission. Like AA meetings, substance abuse counseling, or teams, basketball, hockey. I place all members on one accord.

HOSPITALS

To save lives or treat the ill are the goals of the hospital good deeds. What better reward could there be than to help your fellow man with the compassion of caring.

The recognition you get from working in a hospital comes from within. A feeling of we are all doing mankind a service. A service that allows us to treat the ill, wounded, and suffering. We are not heroes, but we come close.

DONATED TIME

People who donate time for any reason are recognized as great spirits to themselves as well as others. To share what you know, or what you've learned through the years is more then honorable.

POLICING

We are at a time in our lives where multiple forms of Police are needed to Police many different and unique areas. Many areas are difficult area but some Police choose to do this job with out hesitation. We commend them on there service. We understand that the good Officers out weigh the bad ones. Although at times the "Blue wall of silence."

Is silent and creates division among us as a unit front, we still commend you on those good deed done.

EDUCATORS

Every year that passes children are given more rights against what the ultimate goal is. To learn, to be taught by the teacher. Although, some parents expect a babysitter session, and they figure if I drop them there I can enjoy my day. No! School should be an extension of the home. What's taught in school has to be talked about, and figured out, and practiced at home.

Educators are to be commended on their wanting to teach children of multiple cultures, backgrounds, and problems. When they said you couldn't, there was always a teacher who said you could. Look at you now!

HATS OFF FOR THE EDUCATORS!

It takes many good deeds to build a reputation, and only one bad one to lose it.
- Benjamin Franklin

Thinking thoughts is not enough,
Doing good deeds is not enough,
Seeing others follow your good example is enough.
- Douglas Horton

CHAPTER 22

DO IT FOR YOU

If your not different, no one will every say your different. Have you ever realized that those who make it to the top of anything are different from the rest.

Identical twins are different. They may look the same but identify with there own personalities.

Your boss sees who is different in his organization he'll pull them in his office and either offer them a higher salary or a stronger position. It you take the time to look around you will see that most people are just happy to be employed so they keep up with the norms. They don't wanna make any ways. But it's the one that steps out, who dares to challenge the norms is the one who considered different.

The Black sheep of the family derived from the person in the family who chooses to live different from all the rest of the family.

YOUR ANKLES

So you thought you would get mom back for telling you to get back in that tub and wash those dirty ankles again. Mom knew you were destined to become a soccer player. Those hours you spent with the guys in the field kicking that ball around. She knew but she had to let you know she was watching you from afar. That old wash those ankles trick was telling you stay clean because one day those ankles were going to take you to a higher places.

There are many thing in life that people do not for themselves but for others. Sometimes you have to do it for your own self gratification. Because it makes you feel good or better about yourself. You can stop giving for a moment and receive. It would be understood if you leaded back for a spell.

People understand, people with good heart.

You fall in a certain category, the more trusted category. All a person really wants to know about is if they can trust you. Weather they know you or not?

CHAPTER 23
Respect Earned

FROM FAMILY

Family sees you everyday, the watches what you do and what you don't do. They know how you move. Whether you're going to fix something yourself or gonna hire someone because you're to lazy to fix it. They will see if your a man of your word or just talking.

Respect is earned not on the deeds itself but the follow ups. Meaning you got this done because they needed it done. They depended on you to take on the responsibility and you didn't let them down.

BEFRIENDING PEOPLE YOU MEET

You never know who people are that you met on the street. But it does benefit you to grasp something from them. The more people you have come across and collected something from, makes you a power person.

Just imagine being able to tune into anyones conversation. The corner store owner is Indian, I can talk to him because he respects me because of our conversations about his culture. The garbage man respects while everyone else cans are left in the street mine is always neatly placed in front of my car. This is mutual respect learn by a gesture, a simple wave of the hand while turns into a hand shake. We don't know each other but we want the other to know that we appreciate them as a person. "Nothing" more, "Nothing" less.

Courtesy is given, respect is earned.
-Brett J. Talley

Respect is earned. Honestly is appreciated.
Trust is gained. Loyalty is returned.
- Oscar Auliq

CHAPTER 24
PROMISES

A man's word is his bond period!

When the words, "I got you" come out of your mouth only the creator can change what was sanctioned.

FALLING SHORT ON A PROMISE

It's a fact that most people mean well when their trying to assist you with something, buy if you know you, don't have the time, or just can't dedicate yourself then you put me in an awkward position. Wasting my time when I could have gotten someone else instead. We've all received the calls say, "I'm not gonna be able to make it." This goes to the persons character. You should know who they are, and it they truly in their heart could make it or not.

THE LIER

I knew he was lying when he opened his month.

If you are a special type of person and who you may a promise to forgive you for not being able to go through with a promise then you know your second promise must be solid. Strike one is on them, but strike two is on you. Remember, the title "Liar" comes from people who don't keep promises.

DECEIVERS

When they see you coming they already know what you are. You've broken promises with everyone, and they don't wanna hear your lies. The whispering, the silence, you already know what they think of you. And probably don't even care. It's bad not to be trued.

EXCUSES

I was so busy, I forgot! Learn what their telling you. Their were too busy to assist you or they forgot about you. Which means, when you called me I came straight over and I placed my business on hold for you. This means your calling me for a favor is more important than me calling you for one. No more favors from me.

DELAYED PROMISES

The promises made and hope you forget to call back. The "I thought you changed your mind" or "You didn't call me back." If you and I are family or friends we suppose to think, security first for this person, then if they need me I'm there. So if your not there when I need you, what makes you family or a friend!

FAKE PROMISES

He knew when he was telling you that he wasn't going to assist you. He just said it to appease you. Careful of this one, your destined for jail or the grave with him as a friend.

A promise means everything, but once it is broken, sorry means nothing.
- Ernest Hemingway

CHAPTER 25
Your life's treasures

Joseph Campbell stated that there were just three things to teach:

SIMPLICITY - being easy to understand
PATIENCE   - the capability to accept or tolerate delay
                         without getting upset.
COMPASSION - pity and concern for the sufferings or
                         misfortunes of others.

A man may say he's done a lot of things, and met a lot of people in his lifetime, but until he's seen the world through others eyes he's done nothing.

MIND & BODY AS ONE

A mind is a powerful tool but when it connect with a strong healthy body the sky is the limit. You might have heard the term "Mind, body, and spirit." These three components together, as one.

Many try and increase their mind strength by developing skills from other. This will only help strengthen your mind if you read up on it. Many have also tried increasing their body strength by watching someone exercise. I'm not saying none of these techniques don't work, I'm just saying do your homework before your venture. What's good for others might not be good for you.

FAMILY OVER MONEY

Until you gain an avenue to making as much money you want stay close to family. Who ever you consider family. Family are the ones who were supposed to have been around when you had nothing.

HONOR OVER DISHONOR

Believe that what you say and do is who you are. Don't just talk because you have lips and walk away. People wanna know that if you say something you stand behind what you say.

THE VALVE OF A WORD

Use your words wisely. People pay attention to words of power, or words that suit a particular interest of theirs. Caution yourself on using certain words at times of mayhem or distress.

What are your life treasures as stated by Juana la lquana:
    The beauty of nature
    The joy of friends
    The love of family
    The Thrill of learning

It is by going down into the abyss that we recover the treasures of life.

> *Where you stumble there lies your treasure.*
> *- Joseph Campbell*

CHAPTER 26
Alone times

ALLOW YOURSELF TIME TO COLLECT YOURSELF.
There are those who always complain about not having enough time to do what they want to do. They say "Ain't enough hours in a day"! Well if they structured their lives in a way which would be beneficial to them or learned to plan it would help them tremendously. Just stop what your doing one day and say this running isn't for me. I need to slow myself down. Reorganize your thoughts to benefit you. Most of the time people spend more time taking care of other's first, then themselves. How is this possible?

DO WHAT YOU NEED TO DO TO RELAX.
Only you know what makes you happy. What ever it is, this is your me time. Find ways to allow yourself me time in a day.
You will find that in the City areas are different from suburban areas things seem to move quicker in City areas. Your thoughts must move quicker in City areas. You have to be more on point

in City areas. People are different in City areas. Time pass quicker in City area. You can literally be 20 years old and look up and be 35 with three kids. Saying where did the time go! It takes a special person to understand that time waits for no one. Be that special person.

LEARN YOURSELF

If a man says to you that you will never see as much daylight as him try an understand what he's saying. He's actual saying that there's more to you then meet the eye. He's saying don't sleep on yourself you have something that others need to know about you. But you need to unleash it so that you can move on to the next level of you.

Haven't you heard that graveyards are full of people with dreams. Your still here so bring the dreams alive. Learn who you are and project that image and people will understand who you are.

BREATH EASY

It's hard to tell a person to slow down, take a breather because most people don't even know what that means. Most would say yeah I know what your talking about, but do they really. A word from another person should always be taken in consideration. If this person said something that clicks in the back of your mind you already know something is there. Your conscious is ahead of the game. You already knew this but until it was said by someone else now you collect it. It's "a-shame" that we wait for other's confirmation to fix ourselves.

Breath easy only means take breaths to allow oxygen to enter your lungs in a way to relieve your tension. That's it! Nothin complicated. There are all types of methods used to relax the body. One of my favorite is "Box breathing!" This is when you draw an invisible box with you finger, and as you go vertical on the box you inhale, as you go horizontal you exhale. This is done repeatedly as many times desired. It has a relaxing effect on the body both mentally and physically.

The thing is how do you relax if you don't know what relation is. I had a friend who was always moving. He never sat still. Every year he would prepare himself for his annual vacation. He would buy clothes and things for his trip, Uber to the airport and on the plane he went. He'd spend a couple of days came back and complain that he had no money. That meant to me that the entire time he was on vacation he was thinking of his bills. So was it a vacation! Because those bill were there when he got back.

That's not how you breath easy. Don't just do things to impress other or to say I've been on vacation. And I'm not saying don't travel or go on vacation that causes you to travel. Make it make sense. If you gonna relax, then do what it takes to relax. I find relaxations in my backyard. My mind travels to many places and my bills stay paid!

COLLECT & ORGANIZE YOUR THOUGHTS

Many things come to you in a days time. It's better if you arrange each thought in it proper perspective. Don't organize your gym thoughts with your business thoughts.

It's like placing your gym shorts in your office desk. Not a great organization skill. If your all over the place in organizing your life, your life will never be organized. Structure is important. A bike rider who loves riding his bike and keeps it in his room will always be tempted to ride because he sees it on a daily bases. If he is to progress to who he is, he must place the bike in the garage. Then he can fully focus on what he needs to do to get that career going that he visions.

Not everyone can resist the pleasures, and temptations of fun. Fun is a tool to relax the mind so if it's seen on a daily bases those with low temptation meters will choose fun.

Collect yourself would be know what you want your results to be and know that step one will take you to step 2 and so one. The hardest part of life is learning something new. There are those who welcome it, and others who fear change. Pick one! Then you'll know where you'll be years from now.

Oprah Winfrey one stated, *"Alone time is when I distance myself from the voices of the world so I can hear my own!"*

CHAPTER 27
The battle is never lost

An animal will sense many things fear being one of them. It's ok to be scare, but it's how you handle your fear is what makes you. Do you believe that as Daniel entered the lions den he wasn't scared. It was the power behind him that gave him the knowledge, wisdom and understanding to know that as he walked through the valley of death he would fear no evil. Mine you the lions had other things in mind.

GIVING UP

You can choose in life to let the next man fight your battles, or you can fight them yourself. Stand up, the battle start when you say "I have had enough!" I take right over wrong, health over sickness, peace over war, love over hate, and living over dying. The hardest part of this word is staying alive. It's easy to give up and say "I quite!"

On average, most people choose to live expecting a better

tomorrow. This about it!

One of the greatest gift given to a human being is the ability to look forward to another day. It becomes sad when you've reached the age in which your body can no long work as you wish it too, but if you're had glorious memories, and family who care about you, your battle is never over.

THE MUSIC PLAYED

No matter where you are there's always someone who wants your peace. You try crossing the street, they cross. You try walking a different direction, you walk right into them. You go to Church, your coming out they're passing you coming in. Stop trying to avoid someone who has no power over you.

If a battle can't be won don't fight it.
- Sun Tzu

Don't fight a battle if you don't gain anything by winning.
- Erwin Rommel

CHAPTER 28
The foot of the cross

KNOW YOUR PRAY ROOM

For many of years mom's have been the back bone of the spiritual anchor of the family. Praying for their husbands to come home safe from work, for their children to be safe on the street, or just for better life advancements.

These moms had a special praying place that gave the their power to face all obstacles before them. They would knee at the foot of the bed and give thanks first, ask the almighty for guidance. This was not only to ask for guidance and to give thanks, but to stay in line with the creator. Everyone needs to know that there is a power greater then themselves.

SPECIAL PLACES TO PRAY

Although many cultures choose to organize in prayer, prayer can be implemented anywhere as shown in a tragic event. When you are in any type of serious accident or are confronted with a death or someone dear to you your first thought "Oh god" pray for his soul and his loved ones. See, your praying without knowing your praying. Not to mention most peoples last words are that of a prayer. He might not have said that he prayed, but the life he lived that was given to him is now being taken away and he understands that it was given to him by a higher power, given to him to only live.

GIVE PRAISE ALWAYS

They will alway wanna know if you pray. They don't understand that that's between the creator and you. If you took a moment each day to say "Thank you lord", he'll hear you so why do you have to show the next person what they want to see or hear. Give thanks where ever you stand!

KNOW THOSE WHO PRAY FOR YOU

Most of the time you will never know all those who pray for you. But welcome those who you do know. Prayer is alway good from whoever. We already know that you pray for your physical or unearthly enemies to be put in their place. Believe that that enemy is praying for you in return.

EXCEPT THE BLESSINGS

Learn that good things come to good people, but so do bad things. It's a matter of staying away from the bad and excepting the good.

Will your way to excepting all good things. Pray that no bad things come your way. But, if confronted with the negative, pray the negativity away.

I know that all will never agree to what's being said, but in your life time you've prayed for something!

Example: You brought a new car, your hopping it doesn't rain for a few days so you could enjoy it. Your looking out the window saying, "Please don't let it rain!" Your talk to someone!

Most cultures recognize kneeling down to something greater than themselves.

THRUTH TO FACT

The truth is most of us in times of sorrow look somewhere for relief. Could this relief we look to be the higher power?

The grown is level at the foot of the cross.
- Billy Graham

CHAPTER 29
Appearance

As generations progress, appearances seem to demise from what we once knew or change to fallen gestures. How clothes are being worn now may seem disrespectful or even outrageous.
Our African American cultures are subject to changes frequently. We create ways to wear clothing differently. First it was bell bottoms, the wider the pants leg the better. You could hear the flapping when there was a strong breeze. Then there was the pants on backwards which never made no sense. Now, the pants that fall down showing your rump. No body wants to see your rump. I guess we rather them start wearing them backwards again.

Fashion as they call it now can be any trend that catches the eye of the youth. From that fashion they change or enhance it to another fashion. All it takes is one person from every state to see this, and like magic, it's out there. It might turn out to be a fab, it may last forever, or it's a hit or miss. One thing's for sure, the prices of fashion today is nothin like the prices years ago. Why can't we just pump the breaks for a minute and bring back the basics. One dollar t-shirts, nine dollar pants, twelve pair of socks for five dollars. Shucks, even penny candy is a quarter now.

Judges prevent us from seeing the good that lies beyond appearances
- Wayne Dyer

CHAPTER 30
Your chances

Reach, when you were small you had no problem reaching for those cookies on that shelf. You orchestrated a plan to get to those cookies by placing a chair to the counter and maneuved your way around to that cookie jar. Although the chair slipped away from under you and you fell, you still reached for what you wanted.

Life teaches you many lessons. They may not be the ones you desire but you will surely learn from them.

Some people search all their lives never find what they're looking for, others find some what of what they were looking for and learn from the experience.
The point is you will never get one hundred percent of what your looking for so why not try and make you some what happy.
Taking chances and experimenting in life is what life's all about.
Learning from your mistakes and correcting them is important

to getting to know you, yourself. How do you know what you like when you haven't had anything of anyone or compare it to. If I ate only apples all my life and never taste an orange is that fare to you.

What gives a person a sense of their likes, dislikes, is to experiment and have something to compare it to. Don't limit yourself to anything. This world allows you the freedom to grasp what's in your reach and then grasp some more.

Remember, you may get a second chances, but thirds, and fourths, that becomes a wish.

I did then what I knew to do.
Now that I know better, I do better.
- Maya Angelou

CHAPTER 31
Nourish the body

IMPORTANCE OF A GOOD MEAL

As more fast food stores come up we lose our vitamins & minerals. The foods from the earth are being broken down. The body become more fragile, prone to more disease, accidents. We are living in the days of the burger, pizza, Chinese food. A fast food world. Those who care to understand their bodies know that a complete meal of substance is required. Foods of strength and vitality are needed.

Remember the four food groups:
      Proteins
      Grain food
      Vegetable
      Fruits

The food you eat can either be the safest & most powerful form of medicine or the slowest form of poison.
- Ann Wigmore

CHAPTER 32
A kind heart

You'll make it far in the world mentally with a kind heart, but it's not you you have to worry about it's others around you. The ones that know you as having a kind heart. This sometimes causes them to take advantage of you. Knowing you'll be there when they need you, and knowing it's hard for you to say no to them. Learn to flick the switch when it comes to an energy that doesn't feel welcoming.

Not everyone will have the heart you have. Not everyone will appreciate you and what you do for them. Sometimes it won't be easy having a kind heart in a cruel world. Be prepared.

CHAPTER 33
Following others

YOUR SIGHT MATTERS

If you can't see because someone is in front of you how do you move forward? If you've ever been in a crowded hallway and couldn't see the exit because of the people in front of you you'll know what I mean. The world we're looking for is obstacles.

In life there are so many obstacles in your way that some people choose to give up. Not an option for a young or great mind. Others choose to either go around the obstacle in which will take time to maneuver or go right through it. Figure out your direction.

PEOPLE SEE THINGS DIFFERENTLY

Your sight is your sight. No two people see the same. Not even identical twins who share the same egg. The closest you will ever come to seeing what others see is to have the ability to know what another person is thinking. I don't know you like that, but if you can "God bless you"!

BORN TO LIVE YOUR LIFE

It takes some people a lifetime to understand that the life they're living is theirs. We see many miserable, unhappy, painful face looking people everyday. Some are this way because of lack of opportunities, others financially handicapped, due to reasons beyond their control. We also know that the powers that be divided people up into three groups, the rich, the mid class, and the poor. I guess there was a reason for this but who cares. You just need to do what it takes to not end up on that poor end.

KNOW WHATS GOOD FOR YOU

When you walk out your front door in the morning until you reach the end of you day there will be someone who will tell you that something is not good for you. It's cool, because maybe they are a nutritionist, maybe they are looking out for you, or maybe they are just trying to make themself look good. Many do not practice what they preach. They tell you one thing and behind close door do the opposite. It's really not ok because they are hypocrites. But if your persuaded by them without doing your homework, than you get what you get.

When you become a certain age just don't except what people tell you for truths. Their truths are not your truths.

Strong people don't follow the crowd.
Even if the crowds against them.
- Margaret Thatcher

CHAPTER 34
Disgraceful

The idea that a son can say to his mother or father "What have you done for me!"

We'll make it brief, if it wasn't for them you wouldn't be exist. The idea that a child would have his family placed in harms way because of something he did.

The idea that a child would have his Elderly parents come back and forth to visit him in prison for something he did.
The idea that you would even talk back to your parents. Disgraceful!

It is disgraceful to live at the cost of one's self-respect.
- B. R. Ambedkar

CHAPTER 35
Sickness

REMEMBERING COVID

Image by cromaconceptovisual from Pixab

If you have never been sick God Bless you. But if you've been sick with covid and lived through it, God Bless you 3 times over!

WHEEZING IN YOUR CHEST

I can't speak for everyone, but what covid did to the body it got respected. Many of us thought we were invincible. Not! If it were in your chest, and you wheezed, you know what I'm talking about. You turned on your left side and your heard what sounded like people talking. Then you turned to your right side and it sounded like angry people plotting to fight the people on the left side.

COVID

IN CASE YOU WEREN'T PAYING ATTENTION

THE INVISIBLE ENEMY

Last nite we all went to sleep and woke up that next morning and found out that spouse, friend, family members were sick! Died!

REMEMBER:

The drive to work. Leery!

The gas pumps. Untouchable.

Door handles. Deadly.

Hand shakings. Contagious.

Clothes off at the door. Infected.

Mask on the street. Partial protection.

Practicing 6 ft safe distancing. Yelling to talk.

NBA cancelled all games.

Woke up the next morning wit a sore throat .

The Hood was tough but Corona was tougher. Churches, DMV, Malls, laundry mats, mom & pop stores, Barber Shops, Hair salons closed. Recreational places closed.

Supermarkets open (everyone needs foods)
Drug stores (Sold out of mask & gloves)
People create ways to cover their nose & mouths.
Mask become the norm.
People mask design mask for profit.

The year a President was to be Elected.
President takes no responsibility on delayed response.
The President said drink Clorox.
Families together at home figuring things out.
Hundreds ran to their neighboring states.
The FDNY, Police Department, ambulance sirens all around,
busy night & days.

Asthmatic people fall out and some died.
Restaurants closed no family night out.
Parks closed basketball hooks removed.
Sick people being turned away from Hospitals. Covid patients
first.

Dentist not seeing patients
Friends & family in hiding due to being sick.
Doctors & Nurses fight about catching the virus from patients.
Lack of safety equipment for Nurses.
Ventilator shortages though out each state.
Mayor suspends city schools.
Mayor & Gov not in agreement on closing school til Sept.
People still gathering in the streets.

People having parties shut down by Police.

Churches have no funerals.

Bodies being place in truck coolers no room in morgues, funerals homes or Hospitals.

Churches having service contaminating people.

Older people afraid to come outside.

Lysol and hand sanitizers to save the day.

Lysol & toilet tissue prices hiked.

Toilet tissue scarce.

Hand sanitizer in you car.

Hand sanitizer at your front door.

Their comparing the virus to other pandemics, spanish flu.

Hardest it states NY & NJ.

Obama predicted this in 2014.

579,000 plus Coronavirus cases in us, 23,476 death today 4/13/20

Coronavirus cases worldwide pass 2 million 4/13/20

How a vaccine could stop the spread of the virus.

     1. Pfizer BioN Teck.

     2. Moderna or Novavax.

Johnson & Johnson developing vaccine for virus.

The question emerges:

Will COVID be here for ever?

The "We will rise(SPEECH)" soothes the crowd!

REMEMBER THESE TIMES WHEN COVID CHANGED

OUR LIVES FOREVER!

CHAPTER 36
Watch TV (Careful) For Converstion

Ordinarily I would say that tv isn't a great tool for learning, but if you can't stop a person from watching then they might as well learn, get something out of watching it.

All programs have something to teach if your willing to take something out of it.

Different nationalities, and culture learning develops you skills with people. When you can relate to s person about their food, where they come from it's the beginning of an informal relationship. A person will appreciate you knowing something about them. Living in a diverse place as New York and its my cultures the learning will never stop for those who open up to a better them.

UNDERSTANDING PEOPLE
How could you say you understand what a person goes through

when you don't care to understand what the person is telling you.

If I'd listen to my brother I'd know his pain. You should aways tell yourself this because when he is no long around then comes the I should haves, I could have. Be better then the you who thought he knew but didn't.

TECHNOLOGY
Everyone's a fan of television, but what happens when what your seeing isn't what your really seeing.

There are people who would place messages in programs hoping you won't get it. And most of the time you won't because of you having an unaware mined. STAY WOKE

About the Author

Othir Brister, Jr. was born on the 1st day of August 1960 in Sunflower Mississippi; a state known for its hickory, oak woods, grain, super fertile soil, yielding soy beans, sweet potatoes, and other crops.

He was born to achievers Othir and Joann Brister who worked endless hours in cotton fields to ensure their children a better way of life. His parents set their eyes on moving to New York City; soon settling in the Big Apple with their three children. His mom opened up a Beauty Salon, and his pop became a Chef; a job he loved so dearly. Upon saving for a few years, they eventually brought a house in Queens, New York where the family expanded to three boys and two girls. There they all remained until the children began raising their own families. His Pop's heart gave out on him in July of 2018, which they all felt the effects of. So now, everyone stays close to mom making sure she's alright.

They say that a child's earlier years are their formative years. During Othir's earlier years he found that to be true. He watched his mom come from work while his pop headed out to work. So, he learned what work was about. His first job was that of a paper boy. It was an easy job; riding a bike, and throwing papers in yards, occasionally being chased by the neighbor's dogs-so much fun. The job ended when his mom found out that he was being ripped off by the owner. That was just the beginning of many jobs to come, and he had his share.

There were many sports that he was involved in, but basketball was his favorite. Basketball, friends, and the park was his life, along with the night lights. He only went home for one thing - to eat. The streets became his second home, so much that his family often went looking for him.

But, with all the good times, came the bad times. Before he could graduate from public school, a close friend was stabbed repeatedly in front of him during the graduation ceremony. Then, another was shot dead by a gang member. This left a scar!

In his high school days, he learned what team sports were about. He joined the track team with a number of guys from the neighborhood.

His speed increased earning him numerous awards: becoming fifth in the New York State Pentathlon, a Track Scholarship, and for the school a new recreational weight room. So, he set his sights on college. SUNY Farmingdale University was the number one track school at that time. The scholarship made it easy for him to get in. This college would set the blue print to the latter stages of his life. He would meet lifelong friends, and his wonderful soul mate, who he'd marry and have three children with. Inevitably, as a SUNY College, the two years were soon over. He later enrolled in Wagner College, then John Jay College and took special courses with Penn Foster College. He was introduced to a correctional environment as a summer job, while he was in college. Othir became a correctional counselor at Riker's Island Facility. After leaving college, he sought jobs in the correctional field.

He landed a job as a New York State Correctional Officer at Sing Sing Correctional Facility. He also worked: at Downstate Correctional Facility and Fishkill Correctional Facility.

After leaving the correctional field and wanting to remain in the law field, he became a Private Investigator. For numerous years he secretly watched people, their houses, tracked vehicles, located people, and listened to endless stories; a cycle that never changes.

But he can tell you this; he now has tremendous respect for all people; the poor, the incarcerated, the mentally challenged, and especially the so called normal.

Other books by Author:

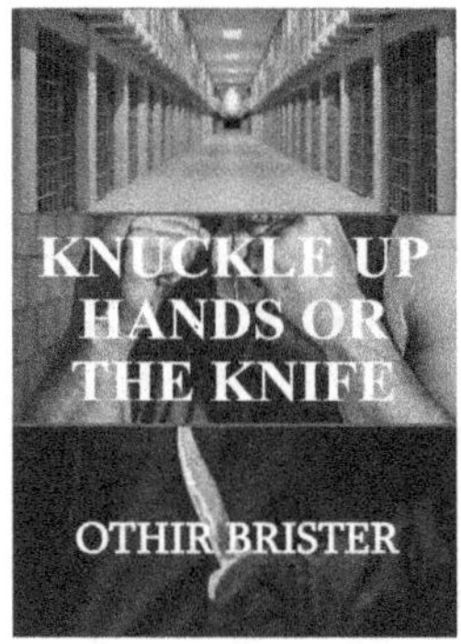

www.ingramcontent.com/pod-product-compliance
Lightning Source LLC
Chambersburg PA
CBHW050753160726
48004CB00002B/541